Axel Scheffler Frantz Wittkamp

FISH DREAM
of TREES

and other curious verses

adapted by
Roger McGough

TW 🦉 **HOOTS**

Warwickshire County Council

ATH 04/8			

This item is to be returned or renewed before the latest date above. It may be borrowed for a further period if not in demand.

To renew your books:

- Phone the 24/7 Renewal Line 01926 499273 or
- Visit www.warwickshire.gov.uk/libraries

Discover • Imagine • Learn • *with libraries*

Warwickshire
County Council

Working for Warwickshire

FISH DREAM of TREES

and other curious verses

There's no bread in the house
Not even a crumb
But cheer up, little mouse,
There's chocolate cake. Yum!

He may look fierce
But he is gentle and meek
This old pal of mine
Who is licking my cheek.

The tiger creeps past
On the tips of his claws
Sees that I'm drawing
So no mighty roars.

Said the old rat catcher,
"When I did trap duty
Rats were GINORMOUS,
Each one a beauty."

Before the end comes the beginning
(With the muddle
Somewhere in between.)
No time to lose!

The giant is gigantic
And just look at Tom Thumb.
The maiden was frantic
When will my prince come?

Those creatures on the mountain
Why do they look so cross?
CLOUD-BITERS they call them
They think it's candy floss.

Winter wind, rain and snow
Soon we know will up and go
Warm whatever the weather
Snug inside a coat together.

Beware the plant that licks its lips
When the two of you are alone.
One day when you've grown nice and fat
It will chew you down to the bone.

No such thing as a wrong tram
Only a wrong destination.
To the poor monkey in tears
This is no consolation.

Once bitten, twice shy
Things will never be the same
Twice bitten, the reason why?
We thought that it was tame.

Smart pigeons realize
There's no need to roam
Or take to the skies
When there's food close to home.

Happiness is a friendly tree
With nobody near.
Sing a song, little bird, for me
Sing it loud and clear.

Very often, hide-and-seek
Is a cruel game to play.
He's been hiding for a week
The seekers, where are they?

We were plant life back in the Plant Age
Vegetables, pulses and grain
Until a human bean took advantage
And developed a voice and a brain.

Fish dream of living in trees
Birds, of swimming in the sea
Humans dream of other places
That they would rather be.

There are some people
Who can't stop growing
Who bang their heads on clouds
(They should look where they're going).

DRAGONS! No creatures
Are as dangerous as these
Yet this one bursts out laughing
On hearing *Big smile . . . say cheese!*

Yesterday it stood straight
Today it is bending.
Sadly for this poorly tree
No happy ending.

Treat a man like a dog
Then take him to the park
Soon he'll fetch sticks
Chase squirrels and bark.

The clown doesn't know
That we're totally bored
But at the end of the show
We'll politely applaud.

Are the swimmers waving?
(In most cases, yes)
Or do they want saving?
(One looks in distress).

"Please don't go away
I will miss you," she cried.
So he didn't row away
But returned to her side.

Did you hear
A broken tea cup?
I thought I heard
An elephant hiccup.

Are they for eating or for wearing?
Are they weapons of war?

The aliens were puzzled
What on earth are books for?

I wanted to buy a raven child
Said the man of uncertain age
But as it's escaped into the wild
Let me purchase the empty cage.

Moon, stop laughing
Keep quiet and let me sleep
I have school in the morning
And promises to keep.

The owl was chewing food
As cautiously I drew near.
"I won't bite," it to-wit to-whooed,
"You have nothing whatever to fear."

There was a hole in my coat
I thought I'd make it disappear
I cut it out with Granny's scissors
(Perhaps not a good idea).

Look, a bear reading happily
No bother, no fuss
If we ask the bear nicely
Will it read the book to us?

Found some cotton
Tied a noose
Caught a lion
Let it loose.

I cough and my bottom is hurting
A smell of burning fills the air
The fire brigade needs alerting
Is it time to rise from my chair?

First published in Germany 2016 by Beltz & Gelberg
This edition published in the UK 2017 by Two Hoots
an imprint of Pan Macmillan
20 New Wharf Road, London N1 9RR
Associated companies throughout the world
www.panmacmillan.com
ISBN 978-1-5098-3650-5
Text copyright © Frantz Wittkamp 2016
Illustrations copyright © Axel Scheffler 2016, 2017
English translation copyright © Roger McGough 2017
Moral rights asserted.

9 8 7 6 5 4 3 2 1
A CIP catalogue record for this book is available from the British Library.
Printed in China

The illustrations in this book were created using
liquid watercolours and coloured pencils.

www.twohootsbooks.com

This little piggy kissed his mummy
This little piggy wiggled his toes
This little piggy tickled his tummy
And this little piggy picked his nose.